MOTHER AFRICA SPEAKS TO CIVILIZATION

Child, I knew you from the first.
When you were but a glimmer in some god's heart,
you stirred inside me, yearning toward dawn.
I knew you when you were without a yesterday,
when all you had were tomorrows,
when your blood teemed wild as the beasts',
and your feet were bare and the earth
was your bed and the sun, your cloak.
I knew you before word or the drum,
before fire or the hunt, before trade or tribe.
I cradled you when the apes mocked
your baldness and then looked on amazed
when you walked erect from the gorge.
Child, you are mine as much as Mount Kilimanjaro,
the Sahara and the Serengeti, as much
as the baobab and the bush. I love the lion,
the zebra, the gazelle and the impala,
but you are my pride. And though you are
my favorite, I let you go out into the world,
for I knew—as well as I know you—
that you would do great things. Keep me
in your heart, and like a long-ago song
whose lyrics are lost but melody lingers,
you will hear me whispering in a language
that belongs to no nation but to all humanity:
Here are your beginnings; here is your home.

REMEMBER THE BRIDGE

POEMS OF A PEOPLE

CAROLE BOSTON WEATHERFORD

Designed by Semadar Megged

PHILOMEL BOOKS

REMEMBER THE BRIDGE

Remember the bridge
that your ancestors crossed,
the sweat that was spilled
and the lives that were lost.
Remember the slaves
who raised corn and picked cotton.
Keep singing their songs
so they won't be forgotten;
the Underground Railroad
that passed through at night,
the signs and conductors
that guided slaves' flight.
Remember the soldiers
who fought though they knew
they might not be free
when the battle was through.
Remember the old souls
who handed down tales,
the bold men and women
who blazed their own trails
from the South to the North,
from farm to big city,
with satchels of dreams
and no use for self-pity.
Remember the bootblacks
who made old shoes shine,
the industrious laborers
who manned factory lines.

8

Remember the housemaids
who scrubbed dirty floors,
the leaders who spoke out
to open closed doors.

Remember the hard way
the ancestors came:
snatched from the Motherland
bound in iron chains.
Remember the voyage,
the capture, the chase,
young warriors who vanished
without even a trace.
Remember the ocean
much too vast to span,
long shadows on shorelines
and footprints in sand.
Forget not the glory
of Africa's past,
the temples and riches
that to this day last:
bronze, baskets and mud cloth,
pyramids of stone,
ebony statues
and bracelets of bone.

The journey continues,
the bridge still holds strong,
hands reach across water,
hearts sing a new song.

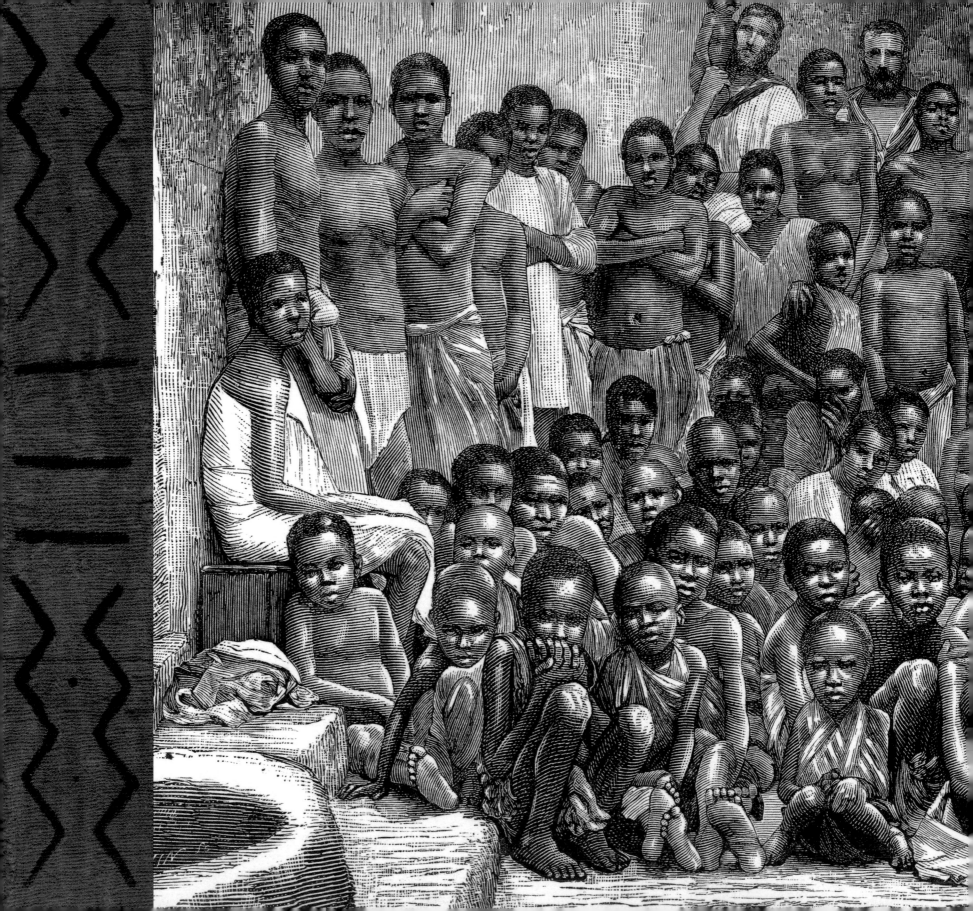

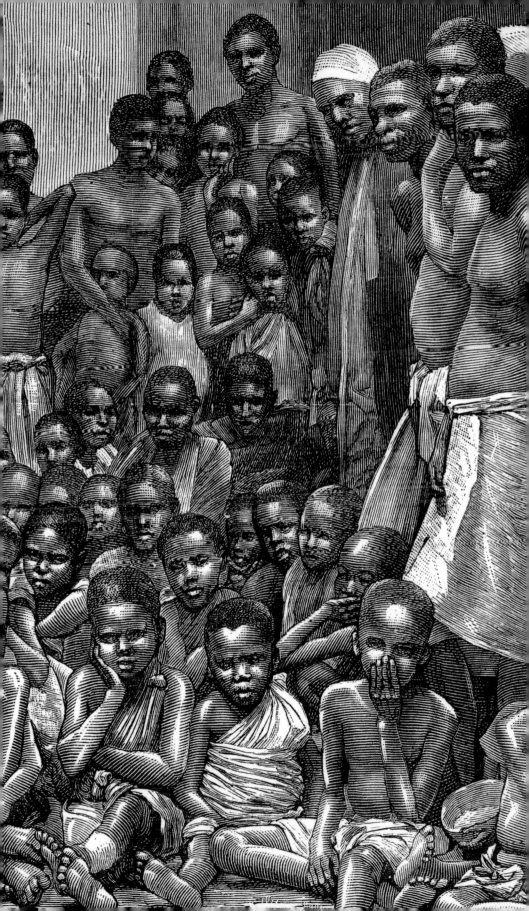

THE CAPTURE

Through tangled vines and dense trees,
Ayo treads a path trod by his father
and his father before him, a path
where he will stare down a lion,
stalk a warthog and cross over
to manhood. Not yet a man,
no longer a boy, Ayo is unafraid.
He will spear the warthog and return
to the village. Drums and dancing
will greet him, and his father
will lead him to the circle of elders.
Pondering the rite of passage,
Ayo does not hear the footsteps
of slavers behind him, the rustle
of ropes that will bind wrists and ankles,
or the clink, clink of trade beads
against rifle barrels. Ayo
does not know that he is hunted,
that he will never be his own man.

OBATUNDE'S NEW NAME

How many days since Obatunde,
shackled and branded, was given
the new name that twists his tongue?
How many moons since he was marched
into the ship's hold and wedged spoonlike
against two hundred other Africans?
Twice daily, sailors bring beans mashed
with palm oil and water, but the stench
of weepy wounds and human waste
makes empty bellies churn. How many
dead thrown overboard, and births
since the ship left shore? Obatunde
has lost count. Time, he marks
by glints of sun through air grates.
Evenings, he is brought to deck for exercise.
The bagpipe fails to lift his heart.
Legs wobbling, Obatunde wonders
where the waves will take him
and why he needs a new name.
Then comes the stinging command,
the cat-o'-nine-tails whipping bare skin.
Dance, Brodie, dance!

13

ON THE AUCTION BLOCK

Ebony skin glistening with palm oil,
arms cradling the son born aboard ship,
the African woman steps up to the platform,
obeys a signal to turn around.
The man with the gavel checks her teeth
and shows the crowd her full breasts.
Then, the bidding starts.
150, 160, 180, 200.
Do I hear 210? Going once, twice,
sold! To the gentleman from Virginia.
A planter with no use for a black baby.
The woman's cries do not stall the sale
of her son. Tears bead up on her cheeks.
Warm milk streams down her bare chest.
Arms empty as her heart.

SLAVES' CHORES

Nettie empties slop pots;
Annie's shooing flies.
Sarah irons the linens;
Cindy's baking pies.
Beulah nurses Little Master;
Esther's spinning thread;
Lucy's fanning houseguests;
Lottie makes the beds.
Patty churns the butter;
Bett shines silverware.
Cathy dusts the woodwork
while Nancy brushes Missus' hair.

Amos milks a dozen cows;
Harry feeds the hogs.
Robert shoes the horses;
Lee is splitting logs.
George repairs the barn door;
Ben makes wagon wheels;
Buck stokes the smokehouse fire
while most slaves work the fields.
Master watches from the porch;
the chores have just begun.
Rising when the rooster crows,
slaves work from sun to sun.

16

THE SLAVE STORYTELLER

Gather round me, children,
behold my native land.
Dream with me of Africa.
The map drawn on my hand
will chart the course through memories,
reveal the roots of man,
deep within a forest
where the drumbeat first began.

Before there was music
or even spoken word,
when the only songs sung
were the melodies of birds,
man turned his ear inward.
A heartbeat's what he heard.
He felt it pitter-patter,
flutter, pulse and pound.
He moved to its rhythms—
throbbing, thumping sound.

From a hollow tree trunk,
a tribesman carved a drum;
stretched hide across its head
and rapped it with his thumb.
The drum echoed through the trees;
tribes called out ancient chants.
The village leaped with glee
in a ritual of dance.

18

JAKE'S PLEA

The mother tongue has left Jake's lips;
he shrieks in silence at the whip.
His shirt is ragged; broad back scarred.
He labors long; his life is hard.

He floods the fields where rice will grow,
yet Master reaps the grain Jake sows.
At harvesttime from dawn to dusk,
he separates the grain from husk.

Running barefoot through the dirt
not knowing they'll be forced to work,
slave children, in the quarter, stay
and, with the master's children, play.

By moonlight, Jake kneels down to pray,
"Don't let my kin be sold away."
This plea, he makes most every night,
then shuts his eyes and dreams of flight.

20

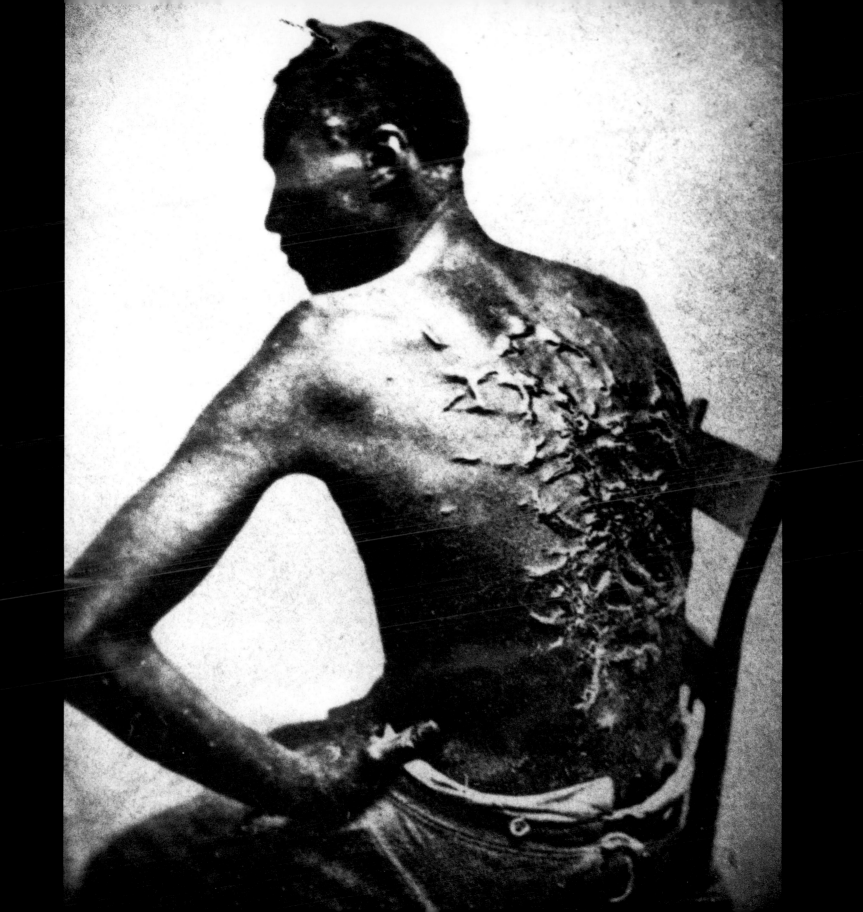

THE CONDUCTOR WAS A WOMAN (FOR HARRIET TUBMAN)

This line ain't got no tracks;
This road ain't got no rails.
Bloodhounds a-howlin'
Huntin' for her trail.

The stations are hideouts;
The conductor holds a gun.
She stops at each plantation
For slaves on the run.

Hear her whistle blowing—
Hoot owl at break of dawn.
Loose those chains and shackles.
Tell not a soul you're gone.

Steal away, steal away
With the rags upon your back.
Run until your bare feet bleed,
Her train won't jump the track.

Won't let nobody turn her round,
She's been through fire and rain.
The North Star is the headlight
On her freedom train.

FAMILY FARM

I raised four sons and sugarcane
on the family farm.
My boys learned how to count
by lugging bushels in their arms.
We plowed a plot to plant our seeds
and prayed that rain would come
and bless us with cucumbers
as green as my right thumb.
We loaded up the wagon
with crops to sell in town;
we shod and groomed the horses
before the sun went down.
Ain't never made much money,
maybe never will.
I trust my dreams
to the rich, brown earth.
My Lord, I'm striving still.

THE BASKET WEAVER

She wades the marshlands and gathers grass
to weave the baskets that hold her past.
She coils sea grass with palmetto frond.
Her timeless art forms tribal bonds.

The craft she learned at her mama's knee,
her forebears brought across the sea.
Baskets sewn with skill by slaves
held grains of rice, and cradled babes.

With pride aglow on her ebony face,
she sells her wares at the marketplace.
The baskets she still weaves by hand
hold memories of the Motherland.

BRONZE COWBOYS

When bison roamed the wild, wild West
dark riders rode the Pony Express
over the mountains, across the plains,
past coyotes, bobcats and wagon trains.
Bronze cowboys rode in cattle drives
where deserts met the turquoise skies.
They busted broncos and bulldogged steer,
made peace with the Indians and showed no fear.
A mail carrier named Stagecoach Mary
fought off wolves on the lonesome prairie.
Nat Love was the surest shot in the land.
Bill Pickett was known as a mean cowhand.
Around the campfire, they strummed guitars,
imagined they could lasso stars.

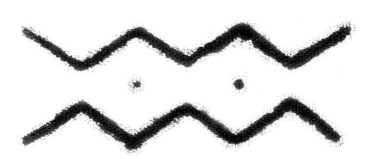

SOUL FOOD

Black-eyed peas, collard greens,
dirty rice and pinto beans,
brown sugar glaze on smokehouse ham,
pickled beets and candied yams;
chicken and dumplings, turkey and stuffin',
buttermilk biscuits and corn bread muffins.
Grandma rose early to prepare this spread,
to bake pound cake and gingerbread,
to shell pecans for Derby pie
and clean a mess of fish to fry.
She asked a blessing before we ate
and always set an extra plate
for an unexpected visitor.
Her home, like her heart, an open door.

29

COME SUNDAY

Papa donned a starched shirt,
buttoned up his vest.
Mama's ribboned bonnet
crowned her Sunday dress.

Me, in my sailor suit
off to Sunday school,
ready with a Bible verse
and the Golden Rule.

On that gettin'-up morning
the choirs clapped their hands,
the preacher hooped and hollered
and sisters fluttered fans.

Hallelujah! Say "Amen."
The spirit made folk shiver.
The church beat tambourines
and marched down to the river.

THE FLAG BEARER

(FOR WILLIAM CARNEY OF COMPANY C)

Across a sandy war-torn shore
the order came for the all-black corps
to charge Fort Wagner; take the lead;
muster courage for the deed.
Six hundred strong that scorching night
pushed ahead to spark the fight.
They marched as enemy fire rained,
a hail that left a bloody stain;
colonel, color-bearer, both struck down;
but the banner never touched the ground.
The flag, one soldier lifted high
toward the smoky summer sky,
crawling over windswept dunes,
dodging blasts despite his wounds.
The tattered flag would tell the story:
the Colored Troops' first stride to glory.

THE MILLIONAIRE

(FOR MADAM C. J. WALKER)

She left the parched fields of the South
but still she lived from hand to mouth,
worked at a scrub board in blazing heat,
washing laundry to make ends meet.

Till dreams bid her to brew her potions,
Madam's line of oils and lotions.
She filled glass jars on the kitchen floor
and sold her wares from door to door.

Her factory ran round the clock,
filling orders for beauty shops:
creams for skin and oils for hair.
Call her Madam—Millionaire.

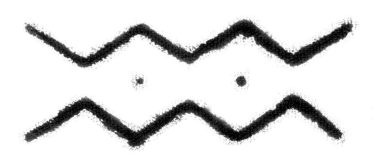

BRAND-NEW ROLLER SKATE BLUES (FOR BESSIE SMITH)

She won a singing contest
at the age of eight
Won a silver dollar singing
at the age of eight
She saved her prize to buy some
brand-new roller skates.

Baby, don't you know
that gal could sing so fine
Oh, baby, don't you know
that gal could sing so fine
She sang her way to stardom
at the age of nine.

The girl left Chattanooga
with a minstrel show
Rode out of Chattanooga
with a minstrel show
She wailed the blues
from Georgia up to Ohio.

She strutted cross the stage
in gowns and satin shoes
Chile, she strutted cross the stage
in gowns and satin shoes
No wonder they all called her
the "Empress of the Blues."

34

THE CONTRALTO (FOR MARIAN ANDERSON)

Banned from playing the concert hall,
she sang outdoors on a grassy mall.
Statues watched as she warmed the crowd,
filling the wind with a sound so proud,
spirituals, arias, from her soul,
rushing, rising as rivers roll.
Praising the Lord and His mighty hands,
her voice, a bell, pealed across the land.
She told America, *I shall sing.*
Listen, children, hear freedom ring!

MISS MAE'S QUILT

The quilt that's draped across Mae's lap
was sewn from old but salvaged scraps
of faded dresses and worn-out skirts,
garments no longer fit to wear
that she cut into strips and squares;
pieces that she cut by hand
to form the patterns that she planned.

On wintry nights her bed is warm
and though frost covers town and farm,
her garden blooms on calico;
stars light a field of indigo.
Each patch holds stories from her life,
her memories, as mother, wife.
Miss Mae now naps in a rocking chair
beneath a veil of snow-white hair.

JAZZ ROOTS

Far, far from Africa
slaves kept the beat alive.
The spirit of the drum
gave them strength to survive.

Slaves breathed their deepest longings
into songs that set souls free,
spirituals, like prayers,
plantation harmonies.

In the muddy Delta,
the slave songs turned to blues.
Singers wailed, guitars whined
on asphalt avenues.
When the blues went uptown
with rowdy razzmatazz,
the sound swelled and swaggered
and swung right into jazz.

The bassist plucked a rhythm,
the cornet blared its call,
jitterbugs were jumping
beneath a mirrored ball.
The piano plinked and tinkled,
the singer tapped her feet;
she wrapped her song in satin
while the drum kept the beat.

39

THE ALL-TIME, ALL-SPORT, ALL-STAR TEAM

Since Ali's the greatest,
let's hire him as coach;
then, we'll draft Jesse Owens.
His long jump wins my vote.
We just might need a big man,
Kareem Abdul-Jabbar.
And golfer Tiger Woods
will finish under par.
We'd better get a pitcher;
so round up Satchel Paige.
Then, he'll call Jackie Robinson
from the batting cage.
Get Florence Griffith Joyner
for her hundred-meter dash
and a pair of tennis players—
Althea Gibson, Arthur Ashe.
Enlist Major Taylor,
he's lightning on a bike;
and running back Jim Brown,
who zooms when he hears, "Hike!"
Catch sprinter Wilma Rudolph,
who triumphs through sheer will.

Tap point guard Michael Jordan
to give the fans a thrill.
Then, ask Magic Johnson
to cast just one more spell:
May all-stars light new stars
and never bid farewell.

DAY'S WORK

Every day at sunup and sundown,
she takes a crosstown bus
to work as a maid and laundress,
to wash and wax and dust.

In uniform of gray and white,
cardboard lining worn-out shoes,
she works so hard to make ends meet,
she hasn't time for blues.

Elbow grease from basement to bedroom,
she spends all morning on her knees
scrubbing till the whole house shines,
even corners no one sees.

In her kitchen cabinet,
a jar of dollar bills.
She never went to college,
but swears her children will.

THE MOTHER
OF THE MOVEMENT

(FOR ROSA PARKS)

The sewing machine hums as Rosa hems
a ball gown; last task before quitting time.
Downtown twinkles with Christmas lights.
She boards the bus, takes the first rear seat
and sighs, hoping she can stay put.
Segregation is a stubborn old mule,
but Rosa stands firm, too. This ride home,
she is not budging for Jim Crow,
not giving up her seat to any white man;
law or no law. Facing handcuffs, Rosa slides
her small hands out of a woolen muff,
wraps her slim fingers around a plow,
and gives that mule a slap. In the soil
of her heart, the movement takes root,
seeds of change blossom, then bear fruit.

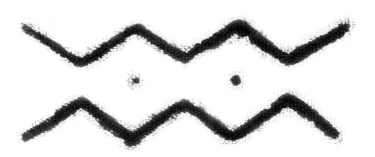

JUNEBUG PEDDLES GROCERIES

Junebug shouts to let folks know
just what he has for sale.
A lady in an apron fills
a paper bag with kale
and plops a dozen fresh trout
in the wagon's rusty scale.

Hard crabs, hard crabs
from the Chesapeake Bay.
Be gone tomorrow—
Better buy 'em today!

Junebug and his pony Belle
jingle through the street,
wagonful of watermelons
crimson and juicy sweet.
The peddler has a ripe smile
for everyone he meets.

44

THE BROWN BOMBER

The radio gave folks a ringside seat
to cheer Joe Louis during his prizefights;
twenty-five titles and but one defeat.
Fans partied past dawn under neon lights
as if their own clenched fists had struck each blow.
They called Joe "the Brown Bomber." He attacked
big, bad opponents, threatened old Jim Crow,
who kept doors closed to hold his people back.
He was a secret weapon in a war
to knock out hate. Joe bore a million hopes
each time he punched a foe. He was a star;
his stage, a mat set off by stakes and ropes.
A left hook, a right jab, muscle and grace;
Joe danced, and pride glowed on every brown face.

MARTIN'S LETTER
(FOR MARTIN LUTHER KING, JR.)

Though sermons rolled off his tongue,
Martin could not find words
to tell his little brown girl
why Funtown's gates were closed to her
or that the "Colored Only" sign
on the drinking fountain didn't mean
the water was a different hue.
But in a jail cell in Birmingham,
he found words to tell the holy men
why he would not halt the marches.
He would rather fight off
police dogs and face fire hoses
than wipe his daughter's tears.

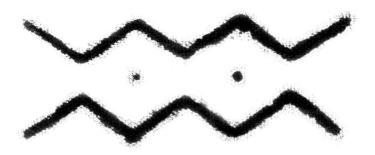

THE EXPLORERS

Esteban set out to search for gold.
Henson braved ice to find the Pole.
Beckwourth trekked beyond the bounds,
and Du Sable settled Chicago town.
They basked in sunsets few had seen
and hiked where hidden springs ran clean.
They forded rivers, bathed in creeks,
camped on cliffs and climbed high peaks.
Bound for glory, compass in hand,
they boldly conquered newfound lands.
Some sailed seas and some rode west,
but one went farther than the rest.
Mae Jemison gazed at this earthly sphere,
rocketed through the space frontier.

FREEDOM FIGHTER

When I think about my people,
I get all fired up inside,
and the rage of generations
moves me like a rising tide.
I've seen the proof of hatred,
men lynched or left for dead.
A stain assaults my memory
with all the blood we've shed.
Someone must do something
and there is no better time,
so I'll reach down in my soul
for strength to speak my mind.
I'll travel north and south
and speak to all who'll listen.
There ain't a man can shut me up,
so lock me in a prison.
I'll put my thoughts on paper
and make clear my demands,
for that which is our due,
our right, in our native land.
I'll stand before the masses
and try to make it plain;
I am an American;
call me by my name.
I'll say what's in my heart
and plead not just for me,
but for my people everywhere
yearning to be free.

49

I AM THE BRIDGE

The bridge is men and women,
famous and unknown,
leaving paths of memories,
timeless stepping stones.
I follow in the shadows
of heroes without names
and keep the faith of elders
who lean on hickory canes.
I hear the beat of Africa
drumming deep within,
bear the scar of slavery
beneath my ebony skin.
I stand with valiant soldiers
who claim the victory
and jump in jubilation
with slaves at long last free.
I rest on sturdy shoulders
of farmers greeting dawn,
carry on the handiwork
of simple folk long gone.
I savor soulful flavors
that simmer way down South
and take to heart the stories
passed down by word of mouth.
I dance to rap and doo-wop
and songs that jazz bands play.

I shout with gospel choirs,
kneel down in church to pray.
I heed the words of protest
that leaders dare to speak;
I march with many thousands,
take my struggle to the street.
The river to tomorrow
is as long as it is wide;
the bridge will get me over,
see me to the other side.
The past is the foundation,
the future the next span.
We'll bridge the mighty river;
brothers, sisters, hand in hand.

AUTHOR'S NOTE

More than two decades ago, I embarked on a pilgrimage into my past. The journey began as a graduate school photo-essay assignment. I had written several poems celebrating African-American heritage and needed images to complement my verses. Though the photo-essay project ended with the semester, my research continued, fueled by a hunger for history. Like a detective, I pored over hundreds of prints and photographs at libraries, museums, historical societies and state archives.

I not only found portraits of famous African Americans but came face-to-face with ordinary folks—farmers, crafters, soldiers, preachers, parents and children—whose identities were long ago forgotten. The images that moved me most were those of slaves taken during the Civil War. Photography was in its infancy, and slavery nearing an end. The faces of slaves spoke volumes about the triumph of the human spirit. Also touching were the photos of families who kept traditions and sowed seeds of sacrifice. Their struggles ushered in progress. While some photos saddened me, my heart danced to the Jazz Age images of legendary musicians in their heyday.

The more I researched, the more photos I acquired and the more ambitious this undertaking grew. After a while, I was no longer looking for photos to illustrate poems, but writing poems inspired by pictures that begged for words. Each image left its mark: a rush of mixed emotions. Sometimes I felt as if I'd entered a museum where the pictures talked. Though I never knew the people depicted, I heard them command, "Never forget; always remember." These poems are their testament.

Carole Boston Weatherford

PHOTO AND ILLUSTRATION CREDITS

Front cover: Detail of "Plantation Family Relaxing on Porch." George Rinhart, North Carolina. © Underwood & Underwood/CORBIS.

Page 4 and back cover: Baobab Tree, Africa. D.V.F. Figueira, between 1900 and 1920. Library of Congress.

Page 6: Five Generations of an African-American Family, J. J. Smith's Plantation, Beaufort, South Carolina. Timothy O'Sullivan, 1862. Library of Congress.

Pages 10–11: The African Slave-Trade—Slaves Taken From a Dhow Captured by HMS *Undine*. *Appleton's Journal* vol. 9, no. 740, 1873. Library of Congress.

Page 12: Gang of Captives Met at Mbame's on Their Way to Tette. *Harper's Monthly* vol. 32, p. 719. Author's collection.

Pages 14–15: A Slave Auction at the South. Theodore R. Davis, *Harper's Weekly* vol. 5, no. 237, 1861. Author's collection.

Pages 16–17: Top row (L–R): "Winding Yarn," *Harper's Weekly* vol. 13, p. 309; "The Cook," *Harper's Weekly* vol. 12, p. 117; "Picking Cotton," *Harper's Weekly* vol. 8, p. 456. Bottom row (L–R): "Ginning Cotton," *Harper's Weekly* vol. 8, p. 459; "Tobacco Plantation," *Harper's Weekly* vol. 11, p. 8; "Gathering the Cane," *Harper's Weekly* vol. 7, p. 760. Author's collection.

Pages 18–19: Zappo-Zapp Musicians, Luluabourg. Author's collection.

Pages 20–21: Gordon, a Runaway Slave From Mississippi-Turned-Union Soldier Under Medical Inspection, Bar Back Showing Scars. McPherson and Oliver, c. 1863. National Archive.

Page 23: Harriet Tubman (c. 1819–1913), Conductor of the Underground Railroad, c. 1880. Moorland-Spingarn Research Center, Howard University.

Pages 24–25: Family Sugarcane Farming, 1930s, North Carolina. North Carolina Collection, University of North Carolina–Chapel Hill Library.

Page 26: Old Woman and Basket, 1890s, St. Helena Island, South Carolina. Southern Historical Collection, University of North Carolina–Chapel Hill Library.

Page 27: Nat Love (1854–1921), Cowboy, c. 1876. Denver Public Library Western History Department.

Pages 28–29: "The Pastor's Visit," from the painting by Richard N. Brooke. *Harper's Weekly* vol. 26, no. 1347 Author's collection.

Pages 30–31: River Baptism. Bayard Wootten, 1907. Library of Congress.

Page 32: Sergeant William Carney (1840–1908), Fifty-Fourth Massachusetts Regiment, United States Colored Troops. *The Black Phalanx*, 1892.

Page 33: Madam C. J. Walker (1867–1919), Businesswoman, c. 1914. Scurlock Studio. Indiana Historical Society.

Page 34: Bessie Smith (1894–1937), Blues Singer. Carl Van Vechten, 1936. Library of Congress.

Page 35: Marian Anderson (1897–1993). Ben-Kow, Stockholm, Sweden, c. 1934. Commonwealth of Pennsylvania, Division of Archives and Manuscripts.

Pages 36–37: Sarah Ann Wilson, American, unknown, United States; New York or New Jersey, Bedcover known as "Album Quilt"; inscription: Sarah Ann Wilson Aug. 1854, needlework, 217.1 x 255.8 cm, Restricted gift of Mrs. David W. Grainger, 1999.509. Photograph © The Art Institute of Chicago. All Rights Reserved.

Pages 38–39: Duke Ellington and Band, c. 1930s. © Bettmann/CORBIS.

Page 41: Jesse Owens (1913–1980), Olympic Champion. Berlin, Germany, 1936. Ohio State University Archives.

Page 42: Mrs. Ella Watson, Government Chairwoman. Gordon Parks, 1942. Library of Congress.

Page 43: Rosa Parks Riding the Bus. Montgomery, Alabama, 1956. © Bettmann/CORBIS.

Page 45: Joe Louis (1913–1981), Boxer. Carl Van Vechten, 1941. Library of Congress.

Pages 46–47: King Feeding His Infant Daughter. Atlanta, Georgia, 1964. © Flip Schulke/CORBIS.

Page 48: Mae Jemison (1956–), First African-American Woman in Space. National Aeronautics and Space Administration.

Page 51: Overhead of Massive Demonstration Crowd. Henry Bacon, Washington, D.C., 1968. © Bettmann/CORBIS.

PHILOMEL BOOKS,
a division of Penguin Putnam Books for Young Readers,
345 Hudson Street, New York, NY 10014.
Philomel Books, Reg. U.S. Pat. & Tm. Off. Published simultaneously in Canada.
Printed in Hong Kong by South China Printing Co. (1988) Ltd.
Book design by Semadar Megged. The text is set in 12.5-point Meridien.
Library of Congress Cataloging-in-Publication Data
Weatherford, Carole Boston, 1956– Remember the bridge : poems of a people /
Carole Boston Weatherford. p. cm.
1. African Americans—Juvenile poetry. 2. Children's poetry, American. I. Title.
PS3573.E135 R46 2002 811'.54—dc21 2001036161 ISBN 0-399-23726-7
1 3 5 7 9 10 8 6 4 2
First Impression

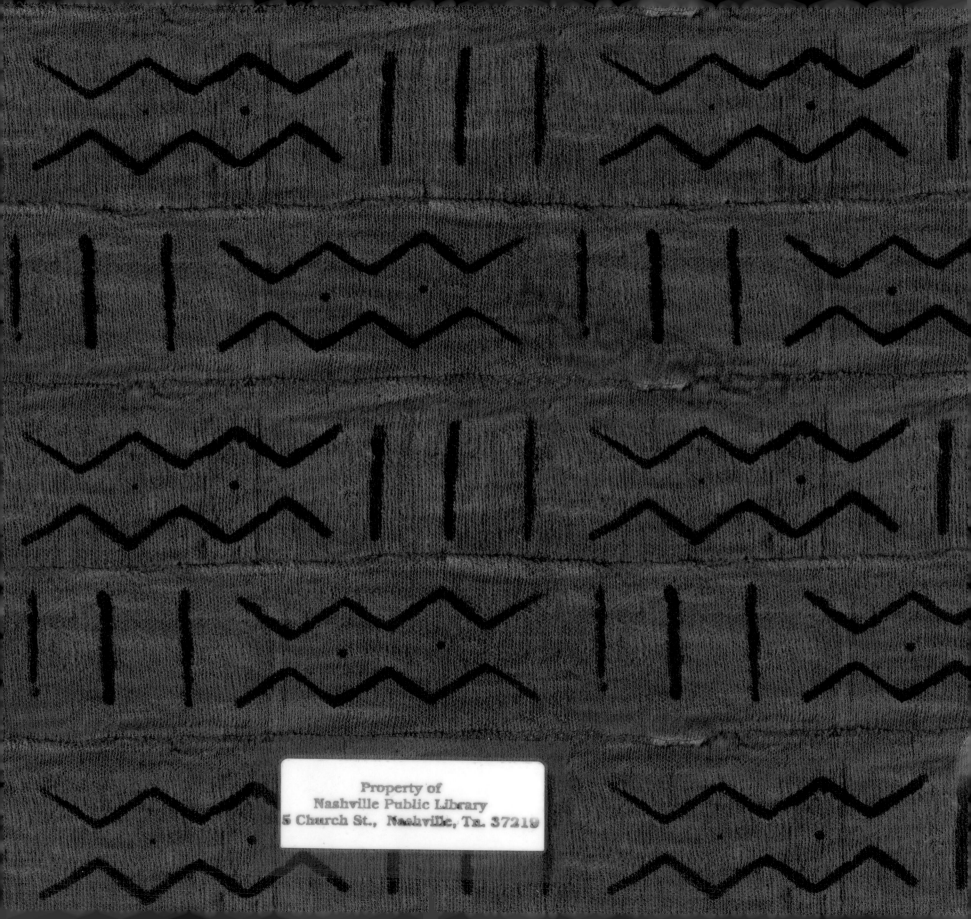